C. H. SPURGEON: THE PRAYER OF JABEZ

IN TODAY'S ENGLISH AND WITH STUDY GUIDE.

GODLIPRESS TEAM

© Copyright 2021 by GodliPress.

All rights reserved. The content contained within this book may not be reproduced, duplicated, or transmitted without direct written permission from the author or the publisher, except in the case of brief quotations embodied in critical articles or reviews.

All Scripture quotations, unless otherwise stated, are taken from the Holy Bible, New International Version (NIV). Alternative versions of Scripture that have been referenced are the New American Standard Bible (NASB) and the King James Version (KJV).

CONTENTS

Foreword v
Introduction ix

1. THE BLESSINGS OF MEN 1
   The Trouble with Flattery 3
   A Prayer of Action 4
   A Final Thought 5
   Study Guide 5

2. BLESSINGS THAT ARE TRANSIENT 7
   Wealth 8
   Fame 10
   Health 11
   Home 13
   A Prayer for Action 14
   A Final Thought 17
   Study Guide 17

3. BLESSINGS THAT ARE IMAGINARY 19
   Imaginary Blessings for the Unsaved 19
   Imaginary Blessings to the Saved 24
   A Prayer for Action 29
   A Final Thought for the Saved 31
   Study Guide 31

4. THE BLESSINGS OF GOD — 33
   Blessings From the Pierced Hand — 33
   Blessings From the Spirit — 34
   Blessings From Your Fellow Christian — 34
   Blessings for Eternity — 35
   Blessings That Help Me Glorify God — 35
   Study Guide — 36

5. A FINAL THOUGHT — 37
   Search — 37
   Weigh — 37
   Pray — 38

References — 39

FOREWORD

This sermon was first published in 1871 as "The Prayer of Jabez." While holding firmly to C. H. Spurgeon's classic teaching and theology and retaining the elegance of his writing style, this edition has been updated to make this sermon more accessible to today's readers.

About the Study Guide

So that you may be able to partake of the blessing that flows so abundantly in these powerful words of Charles Spurgeon, a study guide has been incorporated into the book. This study guide will allow you to truly benefit from his wonderful sermon and bring you closer to this gifted preacher, as he would no doubt have stood atop his pulpit and delivered each and every word with passion, conviction, and a sense of eternal urgency.

About C. H. Spurgeon

Charles Haddon Spurgeon was one of the true greats of the Church. Born in 1834 in Essex in England, young Charles had an in-depth introduction to Christianity, having grown up in a deeply Christian family, then finding himself one day in a Methodist Church, before eventually joining a Baptist Church.

The young Christian was a prolific reader, owning a massive 12,000 volume library at the time of his death in 1892. He grew to be a gifted communicator and preacher. He preached his first sermon before he was even 20-years-old, and it was said that while he had a boyish appearance, it did not match the maturity of his sermons—and those sermons were captivating, powerful, and eloquently delivered.

He was a staunch and committed Calvinist, who nonetheless believed that the greatest truth he could present about himself was that he was a follower of Jesus Christ.

As his sermons garnered him invites to Churches throughout London and England, he would go on to preach to tens of thousands in his lifetime, and while he was an incredibly gifted and therefore popular preacher, he did also have his detractors.

Those who disliked his sermons took issue with their emotive qualities, as well as his tendency to enact Biblical scenes and truths and add a theatrical flair to his messages. Soon, he was being referred to as a "pulpit buffoon," and yet none of this deterred or dissuaded him. Far from it, he used this opposition to spur him on towards greater efforts. He believed that what was of greater importance than being either polite or vulgar as a preacher, was ensuring people listened to his messages; and to that end, he would do what was necessary.

Outside of the pulpit, he left an equally tremendous legacy: He established numerous alms houses, an orphanage, and a Pastor's College which remains in operation to this very day (Christianity Today, n.d.).

About GodliPress

GodliPress exists to glorify God and to encourage believers in their walk with Christ. We do not necessarily endorse all doctrinal views of the authors we publish. Our hope and earnest prayer is that you find our updated editions of the Christian classics much easier to understand and that God would bless you through any teaching in them that is in line with the Gospel as revealed in His Word.

INTRODUCTION

'Oh, that thou wouldest bless me indeed!'
– 1 Chronicles 4:10-KJV.

SORROW FIRST, THEN JOY

We know very little about the man known as Jabez, except that he was more honorable than his peers, and that he was named Jabez because his mother gave birth to him in sorrow (1 Chronicles 4:9-KJV). Sometimes in the order of life, sorrow will always come first, but it is swiftly followed by joy and pleasure.

In the same way that a violent and ferocious storm gives way to the tranquility of clear sunshine, so the night spent weeping yields to the morning of bliss and happiness (Ps. 30:5). Sorrow is the harbinger, and gladness is the prince it ushers in.

William Cowper wrote:

'*The path of sorrow, and that path alone,*

Leads to the place where sorrow is unknown.'

In our daily lives, the reality is that to a great extent we must sow with tears before we can reap in joy. Many of our works done for Christ and in His name have cost us tears and brought us suffering. Difficulties and disappointments have overwhelmed our soul with anguish. And yet those projects that have cost us so much more than ordinary sorrow, have often turned out to be the most honorable of our undertakings. In Genesis 38:18, Rachel gives birth to a son and names him Ben-Oni, (meaning *"the son of my sorrow"*). But Jacob renamed him Benjamin (meaning *"the son of my right hand"*). First, there is the grief or sorrow (Ben-Oni) and then there is the delight (Benjamin). Our base desires can lead to grief, but our faith can bring about God's favor.

You may rightly expect a blessing as a gift from God if you are given the strength to persevere under many discouragements as you serve Him, and against all odds. The ship is often long in coming home because of the many challenges it has to navigate through, such as being detained due to cargo and customs concerns. And yet, how much more satisfying is her freight when she eventually reaches the port?

A MAN OF PRAYER

We are told the following regarding Jabez; that he *'was more honorable than his brothers. His mother had named him Jabez, saying, "I gave birth to him in pain."'* And this young man was not known only for the remarkable circumstances surrounding his birth, but also because of his rather remarkable and peculiar request of God, which was so beautifully articulated, his fame so far recorded and his name so lastingly preserved. More than this, he was a man of prayer. The honor he enjoyed would not have been worth having if it had not been at the expense of great sacrifice, if it had not the result of overcoming great challenges and difficulty, and if it had not been so thoroughly won. His devotion to God was the key to his promotion. Those are the best honors that come from God: the award of grace for the humble offering of service.

When Jacob was renamed as Israel, he received his princedom after a memorable night of prayer (Gen 32:25). Surely, that was far more honorable to him than if it had been bestowed upon him as a flattering distinction by some earthly emperor? The best honor is that which a man gains in communion with his Heavenly Father. Jabez, we are told, *was more honorable than his brothers,* and his prayer is therefore recorded as if to suggest that he was also more prayerful than his brothers.

AN ANALYSIS OF JABEZ' PRAYER

We are told very clearly what petitions his prayer consisted of. From start to finish and all through, it was very significant and informative. We need only take one clause out of it in order to understand the rest: *'Oh, that thou wouldest bless me indeed!'* I commend this as a prayer for yourselves, dear brothers and sisters, one which will be available at all seasons. A prayer to begin your Christian life with, and a prayer with which to end it. A prayer that would never be inappropriate in either your joys or your sorrows.

'Indeed' – True Versus False Blessings

'Oh, that thou wouldest bless me indeed!' The very pith of the prayer seems to lie in that word, *'indeed.'* It's significance adds weight to the prayer. There are many different varieties of blessing. Some are blessings in name only because they only provide a momentary gratification of our wishes, and end up

permanently disappointing our expectations. They charm the eye, but are bitter on the tongue.

Others are merely temporary blessings because they perish with repeated use. For a short while, they may regale our senses and impress us to no end, but in the end they cannot satisfy the higher cravings of the soul.

But, '*Oh, that thou wouldest bless me indeed!*'

'Thou' – What Are True Blessings?

'*Oh, that Thou*'—the God of Israel, the covenant God—'*would bless me indeed!*' I know that whomever God blesses shall indeed be blessed. When God blesses us, the item or object with which we are blessed will be good in itself. It is then bestowed with the good-will of God, who is the loving Giver; and shall then produce so much good fortune for the recipient that it may well be esteemed as a blessing '*indeed*,' for there is nothing comparable to it.

Let the grace of God prompt it, let the choice of God appoint it, let the bounty of God confer it, and then the endowment shall be something God-like indeed. It shall be something worthy of the lips that pronounce the benediction, and to be sincerely craved by everyone who seeks an honor that is substantial and enduring.

'Oh, that Thou wouldest bless me indeed!' Think it over, and you will see that there is a depth of meaning in the expression.

'Bless' – God's Versus Men's Blessings

We may set this in contrast with human blessings: *'Oh, that thou wouldest bless me indeed!'* It is very meaningful and special to be blessed by our parents and those dear friends whose blessings come from their hearts and are backed up by their prayers. Many poor individuals have had no other legacy to leave their children except a blessing; but the blessing of an honest, holy, and Christian parent is a rich treasure to that child. One might well feel it was a thing to be deplored through life, to have lost a parent's blessing. We like to have it, and we enjoy it's fruits in our lives. The blessing of our spiritual parents is a great comfort. Though we no longer hold to any priestly ministry in today's Church services, we do enjoy living in the affections of those who were instrumental in bringing us salvation in Christ, and from those whose lips we were instructed in the things of God.

And how very precious is the blessing of the poor! For those who have the least, offer the greatest and richest of blessings. It is no surprise at all that Job treasured it up as a sweet thing. *'Whoever heard me spoke well of me, and those who saw me commended me,'*

(Job 29:11). If you have helped the widow and the fatherless, and their thanks are returned to you in a blessing, it is no small reward.

But, dear friends, consider this: All that parents, relatives, saints, and grateful persons can do in the way of blessing us, falls very far short of what we desire to have.

A PRAYER OF ACTION

Oh Lord, we would love to have the blessings of our fellow brothers and sisters, the blessings that come from their hearts. However, '*Oh that thou wouldest bless me indeed!*' For Thou alone can bless with authority. Their blessings may be nothing but words, but Thine blessings are effectual. We may often wish for what we cannot do, and desire to give what we do not have at our own disposal, but Thy will is omnipotent. Thou created the world with but a word. Oh, that such omnipotence would now bestow upon me Thy blessing! Other blessings may bring me some tiny cheer, but in Thy favor is life. Other blessings are mere specks in comparison with Thy blessing, for Thy blessing is the title to '*an inheritance that can never perish, spoil or fade*' (1 Pe 1:4) and to '*a kingdom that cannot be shaken,*' (Heb 12:28).

A FINAL WORD

As King David prays so powerfully in another place, '*...with your blessing the house of your servant will be blessed for ever,*' (2 Sam. 7:29).

STUDY GUIDE

The blessing of God is the richest and most rewarding of blessings. After reading Spurgeon's thought-provoking introduction, work through these study questions to gain a deeper understanding of his message.

Take the time to think about each question. Don't rush to the next question if you need more time to reflect and consider. May you be blessed as you study further.

1. "A violent and ferocious storm gives way to the tranquility of clear sunshine." What do you think is the intended meaning behind these words?
2. "Our base desires can lead to grief." What do you think are some of these base desires that Spurgeon warns us about?
3. If our "base desires" can lead to grief, how can some of the works done for Christ also cause us tears and suffering?

4. What do you think should be more important to us, the praise of God or the praise of people?
5. What do you think is the great blessing that God can bestow upon us?

1

THE BLESSINGS OF MEN

Perhaps at this time and at this point, Jabez may have put the blessing of God in contrast with the blessing of men. Men will happily bless you when you do well for yourself. They will praise you when you are successful in business. Nothing succeeds like success. Nothing garners as much public approval as someone who is prosperous and wealthy. The measure of success is the success that can be seen. How sad it is that today's world does not weigh your actions in the balances of the Church and Scriptures but rather in other scales. Our value is seen not in the light of Eternity and the Scriptures but rather in the world and it's flawed values.

You will find yourself surrounded by those who will commend you if you are prosperous or condemn you if you suffer adversity—like Job's comforters and so-called friends. Perhaps there may be some feature about your blessing that will please them because they can likewise benefit from it—and so feel entitled to it. They feel they deserve them. They will commend you for your patriotism because you have been a patriot. They commend you for your generosity because they know of your kindness and compassion. They know that you have aided them and shared with them. And so they understand all too well that your blessing is their blessing, as they partake in it with you. And this is, of course, good, but what is there after-all, in the verdict of your peers?

At a court trial, the verdict of the policeman who stands in the court, or of the spectators who sit in the gallery, amounts to absolutely nothing. The person who is on trial knows that the only verdict that is of importance will be the verdict of the jury and the sentence of the judge. And in the same manner, the opinions, commendations, or even discouragements of our friends and family will have very little consequence or interest for us, whatever we may do or say. Their blessings are not of any great value to us.

But, '*Oh, that thou wouldest bless me,*' that Thou would say, '*Well done, good and faithful servant,*' (Mat 25:23). Receive the feeble service, Holy Father, that I humbly offer from my heart, through Thy grace. That will be the greatest of blessings to me, *indeed.*

THE TROUBLE WITH FLATTERY

We can at times be very excited about what seems like a blessing upon us, but is in fact flattery. In the children's fable by Aesop, "The Fox and the crow," a crow has a piece of cheese in her beak, and once this morsel is spotted by the hungry fox, he flatters her about her appearance and requests a song from her. If she complies, then he would hail her as queen of all birds. And so the crow opens her beak to sing, and drops the cheese straight into the waiting fox's mouth (Kid's pages. N.D.).

There are always those who, like the fox, hope to gain the cheese by praising the crow. They have never seen such beautiful feathers before! No voice could be so sweet as yours! Their interest and concern is not set on you, but rather on what they can get out of you. While the race of flatterers will never quite become extinct, the flattered have usually done a fair job at flattering themselves as well. They may well understand and believe that people flatter often enough, and so can easily identify when they are being flattered, but because they do still see themselves in a rather fair light regardless, they tend to hold that the flattery may perhaps be a little exaggerated, but still exceedingly true!

We are not very likely to take a large discount off the praises that others offer us; and yet, were we to be wise, we should keep close to our hearts those who restrain us and hold us to account. And we should always keep those who praise us at arm's length. Why? Because those who restrain us and engage truthfully and soberly with us to our faces, cannot possibly be making sport of us, but those who extol and heap praise upon us—rising early and using loud sentences to beguile—we may well suspect that there is some other motive behind the praise, which they lavish so richly upon us. And very seldom shall we be unjust in this suspicion, that they have some secret agenda that is invisible to us.

A PRAYER OF ACTION

Young man, are you placed in a position where God honors you? Beware of flatterers. Or, have you perhaps come into a large inheritance? Do you have great wealth and abundance? There are always flies where there is honey. Beware of flattery.

Young woman, are you fair and beautiful to look upon? There will be those that will have their designs on you—perhaps even evil designs—in praising your beauty. Beware of flatterers.

Turn aside from all who have honey on their tongue because beneath all of that honey lies the poisonous venom of a deadly snake. Consider with caution, Solomon's great wisdom, *'So avoid a man who talks too much,'* (Pro 20:19).

Cry now to God, "Deliver me, Thou dear Father, from all this vain adulation, which nauseates my soul." So you pray to Him the more fervently *'Oh, that Thou wouldest bless me indeed!'* Let me have Thy blessing, which never says more than it means, which never gives less than it promises.

A FINAL THOUGHT

If you take the prayer of Jabez as being in contrast with the blessings that come from men, you will then see the true meaning and power in it.

STUDY GUIDE

The blessings of men often follow on your successes, and when those successes are far and few, then their blessings are likewise.

Let these study questions help you explore the blessings of men and the agenda that often prompts these blessings. Read the questions clearly and if there are Scripture references, look them up as well. Do read through the entire chapter where a verse might be referenced to gain a better understanding of the context. This will help you to understand the message Spurgeon is sharing with you.

1. Should we be concerned about our peers thinking well of us or not?
2. Whose blessing should we desire?
3. What do you think you would need to do, in order to receive the blessing of Matthew 25:23?
4. Why should we avoid flatterers? How do you think you might be exploited by a flatterer?
5. What kinds of people should we surround ourselves with?

2

BLESSINGS THAT ARE TRANSIENT

Let us consider the matter from another angle, and compare the blessing Jabez craved with those blessings that are temporal and transient. There are many treasures given to us mercifully by God for which we are bound to be very grateful, but we must not put too much stock in them. We may accept them with gratitude, but we must not make them our idols. And when we do receive and have them, we have great need to cry, '*Oh, that Thou wouldest bless me indeed*,' and make these inferior blessings into real blessings. And if we do not have them, we should cry with even greater vehemence, "Oh that we may be rich in faith. And if not blessed with these external favors, then may we be blessed spiritually. Then we shall be blessed indeed." Let us now consider four such temporal and transient blessings:

WEALTH

Let us review some of these blessings and just say a word or two about them. One of the first cravings of men's hearts is wealth. So universal is the desire to gain it, that we might almost say it is a natural instinct. How many of us think that if we just possessed it, then we would be blessed indeed? But there are ten thousand proofs that happiness does not consist in the abundance of what a person possesses. So many instances are well-known to you all that I do not need to quote any to show that riches are indeed not a blessing. They are more of a false reality than a truthful one.

Hence, it has been well said that when we see how much someone has, we envy them. However, if we could see how little enjoyment they receive from what they have, we would then pity them. Some, who have had the easiest and most favorable circumstances in life, have the most uneasy and fragile minds. Those who have acquired all that they could possibly wish for should have rather directed those wishes towards less self-absorbed ends. And now they are discontented and dissatisfied because they can have no more. Familiarity with splendor and wealth often leads to wanting more and more of the same. When you have, you will always find yourself wanting more and more.

'Thus the base miser starves amidst his store, Broods o'er his gold, and griping still at more, Sits sadly pining, and believes he's poor.'

There is nothing clearer or more obvious to those who choose to observe the truth than the fact that riches do not send sorrow or unhappiness packing. Riches do not attract endless joy, nor do they secure eternal happiness. More often than not, wealth deceives the owner. Delicacies are spread on their table, but their appetite fails. Minstrels await their bidding, but their ears are deaf to all the strains of music. Holidays may come as often as fancy may spark, but recreation, adventure, and relaxation has lost all of its charms. Or, put yet another way, the young gain tremendous fortune by way of a sizable inheritance, and so they make pleasure their pursuit, until even pleasure becomes meaningless and loses all of its efficacy. How easily the wealthy can become disillusioned with their wealth and all that it can afford them.

Riches can so easily make themselves wings, and like the bird that roosts in the tree, they fly away fast and without any sense of loyalty. In sickness and sadness, these riches that seem so capable of nurturing us and saving us offer only empty promises, whispering to us *'Take life easy; eat, drink and be merry,'* (Luk 12:19). In truth, riches prove themselves to be poor comforters. In death, they even tend to make the pang of separation more acute because the more there is to leave, the more there is to lose.

FAME

Another transient blessing which our poor humanity fondly covets and eagerly pursues is fame. In this respect, we would gladly want to appear more honorable than our peers, and outshine all our competitors. It seems natural to all of us to wish to make a name for ourselves and gain some measure of popularity and significance in the circles in which we move. And if we can make that circle wider, then even better.

But here, as with riches, there is no disputing that the greatest fame does not bring with it any equal measure of gratification and happiness. People seeking after notoriety or honor enjoy a degree of pleasure in the search, which they do not always possess when they have gained the object of their search. Some of the most famous people in the world have also been the most wretched of the human race.

HEALTH

There is another temporal blessing which wise men desire, and may legitimately wish for rather than the other two: the blessing of health. Can we ever prize it sufficiently? To trifle with such a treasure is the madness of folly. The highest praise that can be placed on health would not be extravagant. Those who have a healthy body are infinitely more blessed than those who are sickly, regardless of how wealthy they may be.

If I have health, my bones are well set, and my muscles are well strung; and if I scarcely know any ache or pain, but can rise in the morning, and with a spring in my step go forth into the world; and if I cast myself upon my bed at night, and sleep the sleep of the happy—yet, let me not glory in my strength. Because the truth is that in a fraction of a moment it may fail me. A few short weeks can reduce a strong and healthy person to a skeleton. Disease may set in, and the cheek may pale with the shadow of death. Let the strong man not glory in his strength. The Lord *'does not delight in the strength of the horse; He does not take pleasure in the legs of a man,'* (Ps. 147:10 NASB).

And let us not boast concerning these things. Rather, if you are in good health say, "My God, bless me indeed. Give me a healthy soul. Heal me of my spiritual diseases. Jehovah Rophi, come and purge out the leprosy that is in my heart by nature. Make me healthy in the heavenly sense, that I may not be left outside among the unclean, but rather be allowed to stand amongst the congregation of Thy saints. Bless my bodily health to me that I may use it rightly, spending the strength I have in Thy service and to Thy glory. Otherwise, even though I may be blessed with health, I may not be blessed indeed."

Some of you, dear friends, do not possess the great treasure of health. Wearisome days and nights are appointed to you. Your bones have become an almanac in which you note the changes of the weather. There is much about you that is designed to invite pity. But I pray that you may have the blessing indeed, and know what that is.

I can heartily sympathize with a sister that said to me the other day, "I had such nearness to God when I was sick, such full assurance, and such joy in the Lord. I regret to say I have lost it now. I could almost wish to be ill again, if thereby I might have a renewal of my communion with God." I have oftentimes looked gratefully back to my days of illness. I am certain that I have never grown in grace half as much as I have when I have been unwell, and cast upon the bed of pain. It ought not to be so. Our joyous blessings from God should be great fertilizers to our spirit; but too often our griefs are more salutary than our joys are. The pruning knife is then best for some of us.

HOME

I will offer one more temporal blessing, which is very precious—I mean the blessing of home. I do not think anyone can ever prize it too highly or speak too well of it. What a blessing it is to have the fireside, and all the dear relationships that gather around the fireside. The word 'home'—that is, wife, children, father, mother, brother, sister! There are no songs in any language that are more full of music than those dedicated to 'Mother.' We heard a great deal about the German 'Fatherland' half a century ago. And perhaps we liked the sound of a 'fatherland.' But the word 'Father' is the most important part of the word. The 'land' is nothing really. The 'Father' is the key.

There are many of us—I hope—who are blessed with a great many of these relationships. Do not let us become content to satisfy our souls with ties that must before long be severed. Let us ask God that over and above these relationships may come the blessing indeed. "Dear God, I thank Thee for my earthly father, but I do pray that Thou be my Father. For then I am truly blessed indeed. I thank Thee, my God, for a mother's love; but I ask that Thou comfort my soul as a mother comforts her child. For then I am truly blessed indeed. I thank Thee, Savior, for the marriage bond; but I ask that Thou be the bridegroom of my soul. I thank Thee for the tie of brotherhood; but I ask that Thou be my brother born for adversity, bone of my bone and flesh of my flesh. The home that Thou has given me, I do prize greatly and thank Thee for daily. However, I would sooner dwell in the house of the Lord forever, and be a child that never wanders from my Father's house with its many mansions, even though my feet may desire to travel wherever."

You can thus be blessed indeed. If you do not live under the paternal care of the Almighty, then even the blessing of a home, with all its sweet and familiar comforts, will not be equal to the blessing which Jabez desired for himself.

A PRAYER FOR ACTION

About Wealth:

We may well say, if we have wealth, "My God, may I never fall for such hollow trappings. Let me never make a god of the silver and the gold, the coin, or the investment. Let me never adore that which I own—my belongings, assets, estates, and all other possessions, which Thou hast given me in Thy providence. I ask Thee to *'bless me indeed.'* As for these worldly possessions, they will be my ruin unless I have Thy grace with them."

And if you do not have wealth—and most likely most of us will never have it—you may well say, "My Father, Thou have denied me this outward and worldly good. Now, enrich me with Thy love. Give me the gold of Thy favor, *'bless me indeed.'* Then, give to others whatever Thou wish. Thou shall provide my portion and my soul shall wait upon Thy daily will. Do Thou bless me indeed, and I shall be content."

About Fame:

If you have honor and fame, accept it, but let this prayer go up, "My God, may Thou bless me indeed, for what would it profit me if my name were in a thousand mouths, but Thou has spit it out of Thy mouth? What would it matter if my name were written on marble, but not in the Lamb's Book of Life? These blessings are in name only, they are empty blessings. They are like the wind, where you hear the sound but there is no substance. They are blessings that mock me. Give me Thy blessing, then the honor which comes from Thee will make me blessed indeed."

And if you happen to have lived in obscurity, and have never managed to be added to the lists for honors among your fellows, then be content to run your own course well, and fulfill your own vocation. To lack fame is not the most grievous of ills; it is worse to have fame like the snow—it whitens the ground in the morning, and disappears in the heat of the day. What difference does it make to a dead person that people are talking about them? Get your blessing indeed.

About Health:

Whatever you have to suffer, whether weakness, debility, pain, or anguish, may you be so well comforted by the divine presence, that this light affliction may produce for you '*an eternal glory that far outweighs them all,*' (2 Co 4:17), so that you may be blessed indeed.

About Home:

Do I address any here that are separated from friends and family? I know some of you have left behind painful relations and memories, like graves where parts of your heart have been buried. And what remains is bleeding with just so many wounds. May the Lord bless you indeed! To the widow, your husband is your Creator. To the fatherless, He has said, '*I will not leave you as orphans; I will come to you,*' (Jn. 14:18). If all your relationships are made up in Him, then you will be blessed indeed!

A FINAL THOUGHT

I have perhaps taken too long a time in mentioning these temporary blessings, so let me set the text in another light. I trust we have had human blessings and temporary blessings to fill our hearts with gladness, but not to foul our hearts with worldliness or to distract our attention from the things that belong to our everlasting welfare.

STUDY GUIDE

As the great hymn reminds us, there are many blessings; count them one by one! They come straight from the throne and can either uplift us or hamper us when we focus too much on them.

Before starting each study guide, do come before the Lord in prayer. Seek His will and guidance in answering the questions, and get a deeper understanding of the chapter and material.

1. "Riches are indeed not a blessing." Do you

agree with this statement? Please explain the reason behind the answer you gave.
2. How do you think the wealthy can become disillusioned with their wealth?
3. How can an easy life without complication or obstacle, result in a fragile mind?
4. What do you think is the attraction in being famous?
5. In the end, should we rely on our physical health as an example of our blessings?
6. What health should actually concern us and should be our focus?

3

BLESSINGS THAT ARE IMAGINARY

Let us proceed, thirdly, to speak of imaginary blessings. There are such as these in the world, and our prayer is that God may deliver us from them. '*Oh, that thou wouldest bless me indeed!*' We will begin by considering these blessings from two perspectives; that of the unsaved and that of the saved—the non-Christian and the Christian.

IMAGINARY BLESSINGS FOR THE UNSAVED

Self-Righteousness

Take the Pharisee. He stood in the Lord's house, and he thought he had the Lord's blessing. It made him very bold, and he spoke with flattering and gratuitous self-complacency, *'God, I thank you, that I am not like other men'* (Luk 18:11), and so on. He had the blessing, and no doubt he supposed himself to have merited it. He had fasted twice in the week, paid tithes of all that he possessed—even the change in his pocket. He felt he had done everything. His was the blessing of a quiet or a quiescent conscience—a good and easy-going fellow.

He was a pattern for the Church. It was a pity everybody did not live as he did. If they had, they would not have needed any police. Everyone would have behaved accordingly. Pilate might have dismissed his guards and Herod his soldiers. He was just one of the most excellent persons that ever breathed. He adored the city of which he was a proud member and esteemed official!

But of course, he was not blessed indeed. This was all his own misplaced arrogance. He was a mere wind-bag, nothing more. And the blessing, which he fancied, had fallen upon him, had in fact never come. The poor public worker whom he regarded as accursed, went to his home justified rather than he. The blessing had not fallen on the man who thought he had it.

Self-Assurance

Another form of imaginary blessing is found in the person who would scorn to be thought of as self-righteous. They despise the accusation. Their delusion, however, is the same. Theirs is not a self-righteousness, but rather a false righteousness. I can hear them singing that great hymn in Church,

'I do believe, I will believe

That Jesus died for me,

And on his cross he shed his blood,

From sin to set me free.'

You believe it, you say? You believe the Gospel? You believe that Jesus died for you? But how do you know? Upon what authority do you make sure? Who told you?

"Oh, I believe it," they may say.

Yes, but we must mind what we believe. Have you any clear evidence of a special interest in the blood of Jesus? Can you give any spiritual reasons or personal testimony for believing that Christ has set you free from sin? I am afraid that some have a hope that has no ground, like an anchor without any fluke (the sharp grappling ends of the anchor that secures it to something). These people have nothing to grasp, nothing to lay hold upon. They say they are saved, and they stick to it that they are, and think it wicked to doubt it; but yet they have no reason to warrant their confidence.

When the sons of Kohath prepared the ark, and touched it with their hands, they did rightly (Num 4:4-6, 15); but when Uzzah touched it, he died (2Sa 6:6-7). There are those who are ready to be fully assured, and then there are others to whom it will only be death to talk of it. There is a great difference between presumption and full assurance. Full assurance is reasonable—it is based on solid ground. Presumption takes for granted, and with a brazen face claims what it has no real right to claim at all.

A Prayer for Action

For the Self-Righteous

Dear Father, let every one of us feel the sting of this rebuke, and pray, "Great God, save us from imparting to ourselves a righteousness that we do not possess. Save us from wrapping ourselves up in our own rags, and fancying that we have put on wedding garments. Bless me indeed. Let me have true righteousness. Let me have the true worthiness that Thou canst accept, even that which is of faith in Jesus Christ."

For the Self-Assured

I pray you will beware of presuming that you are saved. If with your heart you trust in Jesus, then you are saved; but if you are merely saying, "I trust in Jesus," it will not save you. If your heart has been renewed—if you shall hate the things that you once loved, and love the things that you once hated, and if you have really repented, if there is a thorough and true change of mind in you and if you truly are born again—then you have reason to rejoice. But, if there is no vital change, no inward godliness, if there is no love for God, no prayer, no work of the Holy Spirit—then you saying, "I am saved," is but your own fantasy. It may delude you, but it will not deliver you.

Our prayer ought to be, *'Oh that Thou wouldest bless me indeed,'* with real faith, with real salvation, with the trust in Jesus that is essential for faith, not with the conceit that gives rise to credulity.

A Final Thought for the Unsaved

I have met with people who said, "I believe I am saved because I dreamt about it." Or, "Because I had a text of Scripture that applied to my own case." Or, "Such and such a good man said so and so in his sermon." Or, "Because I burst into tears, weeping and was excited, and felt as I have never felt before."

In truth, nothing will stand the test but this, "Do you renounce all confidence in everything but the finished work of Jesus, and do you come to Christ to be reconciled in Him to God?"

If you do not, then your dreams, visions, and fancies are nothing but dreams, visions, and fancies. They will not serve you in any way when you will most need them too. I pray the Lord to bless you indeed, for of that precious truth in all our walk and talk there is a great scarcity.

IMAGINARY BLESSINGS TO THE SAVED

Too many I am afraid, even of those who are saved —saved for time and eternity—need this caution, and have good cause to pray this prayer. This is so that they may learn to make a distinction between some things which they think to be spiritual blessings, and others things which are true blessings indeed. Let me show you what I mean.

Not as I Will

Is it a true blessing to get an answer to your prayer after your own heart and will? I always like to qualify my most earnest prayer with, 'Not as I will, but as you will,' (Mat. 26:39). Not only should I do it, but I like to do it, because otherwise I might ask for something which might be dangerous for me to receive, or a hindrance to me. God might give it to me in anger, and I might find little sweetness in the giving, but much soreness in the grief it causes me.

I hardly like to repeat the old story of the good woman whose son was ill—a little child near death's door. She begged the minister, a Puritan, to pray for his life. He did pray very earnestly, but he put in, "If it is Thy will, save this child." The woman said, "I cannot bear that: I must have you pray that the child shall live. Do not put in any ifs or buts."

"Woman," said the minister, "... it may be you will live to regret the day that ever you wished to set your will up against God's will." Twenty years afterwards, she was carried away in a fainting fit from under Tyburn gallows-tree, where that very son who was healed was put to death as a felon under the hangman's noose. Although she had lived to see her child grow up to be a man, it would have been infinitely better for her had the child died, and infinitely wiser had she left the decision to God's will. Do not be quite so sure that what you think is a good answer to prayer is any proof of divine love. It may leave much room for you to seek the Lord, saying, '*Oh, that thou wouldest bless me indeed!*'

Broken in Spirit

Sometimes great exhilaration of spirit and liveliness of heart—even though it be religious joy—may not always be a blessing. We delight in it, and sometimes when we have had gatherings for prayer here at the house, the fire has burned and our souls have glowed! We felt at the time how we could sing the great hymn,

'My willing soul would stay

In such a frame as this,

And sit and sing herself away

To everlasting bliss.'

So far as that was a blessing, we are thankful for it; but I should not like to set such seasons up, as if my enjoyments were the main token of God's favor. Or, as if they were the chief signs of His blessing.

Perhaps it would be a greater blessing to me to be broken in spirit, and laid low before the Lord at the present time. When you ask for the highest joy, and pray to be on the mountain with Christ, remember it may be as much a blessing—yes, a blessing indeed—to be brought into the Valley of Humiliation, to be laid very low and constrained to cry out in anguish, "Lord, save me, or I perish!"

Humbled and Maimed

Dear friends, have we not sometimes envied those persons that are always calm, unruffled, and are never perturbed in mind? Well, there are Christians whose evenness of temper deserves to be emulated. And as for that calm repose, that unwavering assurance, which comes from the Spirit of God, it is a very delightful attainment. But I am not sure that we ought to envy anybody's lot because it is more tranquil, or less exposed to storms and tempest, than our own.

There is a danger of saying, *'Peace, peace,'* where there is no peace (Jer 6:14), and there is a calmness that arises from callousness. Deceivers there are, who deceive their own souls. "They have no doubts," they say, but it is because they have done little heart-searching. They have no anxieties because they have not much enterprise nor any pursuits to stir them up. Or it may be that they have no pain because they have no life. Better to go to heaven humbled and maimed, than to go marching on in confidence down to hell. *'Oh that thou wouldest bless me indeed!'*

An Established Builder

Equally, too, with regard to our work and service, I think our prayer should always be, *'Oh, that thou wouldest bless me indeed!'* It is sad to see the work of some good men—though it is not ours to judge them—and discover how very pretentious and how unreal they are. It is really shocking to think how some men pretend to build up a church in the course of two or three evenings. They will report, in the corner of the newspapers, that there were forty-three persons convinced of sin, and forty-six justified, and sometimes thirty-eight sanctified. I do not know what besides such wonderful statistics they give as to all that is accomplished.

I have observed congregations that have been speedily gathered together, and great additions have been made to the church all of a sudden. And what has become of them? Where are those churches at the present moment? The dreariest deserts in Christendom are those places that were fertilized by the patent manures of certain revivalists or evangelists. The whole church seemed to have spent its strength in one rush and effort after something, and it ended in nothing at all. They built their fancy wooden house, piled up the hay, and made a stubble spire that seemed to reach the heavens—and there fell one spark and all went up in smoke.

And he that came to take over the job—the successor of the so-called "great builder"—had to get the ashes swept away before he could do any good. The prayer of every one that serves God should be,

'Oh, that thou wouldest bless me indeed.' Plod on, plod on. If I only build one piece of masonry in my life, and nothing more, if it be gold, silver, or precious stones, it is a good deal for a man to do. Of such precious stuff as that, to build even one little corner that will not show, is a worthy service. It will not perhaps be spoken of much, but it will last. And that is the point: It will last!

A PRAYER FOR ACTION

For Those Praying Not as I Will

You remember how Israel of old asked for meat, and God gave them quails; but while the meat was still in their mouths, the wrath of God came upon them. Ask for the meat if you like, but always put it like this: "Lord, if this is not a real blessing, do not give it to me." In other words, "Bless me indeed."

For the Broken in Spirit

Pray with me, this poem by my own hand:

'If today He deigns to bless us

With a sense of pardon'd sin,

He tomorrow may distress us,

Make us feel the plague within,

All to make us

Sick of self, and fond of Him.'

For the Humbled and Maimed

My God, I will envy none for their gifts or graces, nor their inward mood or outward circumstances —if only Thou would *'bless me indeed.'* I would not be comforted unless Thou comforts me. Nor would I have any peace, but Christ my Peace. Nor any rest, but the rest that comes from the sweet savor of the sacrifice of Christ. Christ shall be all in all, and none shall be anything of value to me save Christ, Himself.

Oh, that we might always feel that we are not to judge the manner of the blessing, but must leave it with God, to give us what He would have us receive, not the imaginary blessing or the superficial and deceptive blessing, but the true blessing indeed!

For the Builder

'Establish the work of our hands for us—yes, establish the work of our hands,' (Ps. 90:17). If we are not builders in an established church, it is of little use to try at all. What God establishes will stand, but what men build without His establishment will certainly come to nothing. *'Oh, that thou wouldest*

bless me indeed!' Sunday-school teacher, let this be your prayer; usher, local preacher—whatever you may be—dear brother or sister, whatever your form of service, do ask the Lord that you may not be one of those plaster builders using sham materials that only require a certain amount of frost and weather to make it crumble to pieces. May it be yours if you cannot build a cathedral, to build at least one part of the marvelous temple that God is building for eternity, which will outlast the stars.

A FINAL THOUGHT FOR THE SAVED

These variable experiences of ours may be blessings indeed to us, and had we been always rejoicing, we might have been like Moab, settled on our leftovers, and not emptied from vessel to vessel. It fares ill with those who have made no changes in their lives; they do not fear God.

STUDY GUIDE

Blessings that interest us but focus only on ourselves and our own well-being have less to do with God's will, and more to do with our own wants and desires.

If you are using the study guide in a group, encourage each person to share their answers to the questions, as this allows for a range of different perspectives. If you prefer to enjoy the guide on your own, then take the time to do research on the different concepts and ideas.

1. What do you believe it means to be self-righteous?
2. What is the difference between saying Jesus is Lord and believing in your heart that Jesus is Lord?
3. Why is it important for Christians to pray *'Not as I will, but as you will?'*
4. Does an answered prayer in our favor mean we have secured God's will?
5. How can suffering, adversity, and humiliation bring us closer to God?

4

THE BLESSINGS OF GOD

I have one thing more to mention before I bring this sermon to a close. The blessings of God's grace are true blessings indeed, which, in truth, we ought to seek after. By these marks shall you know them.

BLESSINGS FROM THE PIERCED HAND

Blessings, indeed, are such blessings as come from the pierced hand; blessings that come from Calvary's bloody tree, streaming from the Savior's wounded side. Your pardon, your acceptance, your spiritual life, your oneness with Christ, and all that comes of it—these are blessings indeed.

BLESSINGS FROM THE SPIRIT

Any blessing that comes as the result of the Spirit's work in your soul is a blessing indeed; though it humbles you and though it wounds you. Though it kills you, it is a blessing indeed. Though the plough goes over and over your soul, and the deep plough cuts into your very heart; though you be maimed and wounded, and left for dead, yet if the Spirit of God does it, it is a blessing indeed. If He convinces you 'in regard to sin and righteousness and judgment' (Jn. 16:8), even though you have not yet been brought to Christ, it is a blessing indeed. Anything that He does, accept it. Do not be doubtful of it, but pray that He may continue His blessed operations in your soul.

BLESSINGS FROM YOUR FELLOW CHRISTIAN

Whoever leads you to God is in like manner a blessing indeed. Riches may not do it. There may be a golden wall between you and God. Health will not do it; even the strength and marrow of your bones may keep you at a distance from your God. But anything that draws you nearer to Him, is a blessing indeed. And if it be a cross that raises you, if it raises you to God, it shall be a blessing indeed.

BLESSINGS FOR ETERNITY

Anything that reaches into eternity, with a preparation for the world to come. Anything that we can carry across the river, the holy joy that is to blossom in those fields beyond the swelling flood, the pure cloudless love of the brotherhood, which is to be the atmosphere of truth forever—is a blessing indeed. Anything of this kind that has the eternal broad arrow on it, the immutable mark, is a blessing indeed.

BLESSINGS THAT HELP ME GLORIFY GOD

And anything which helps me to glorify God is a blessing indeed. If I am sick, and that helps me to praise Him, it is a blessing indeed. If I am poor, and I can serve Him better in poverty than in wealth, it is a blessing indeed. If I am in contempt, I will rejoice in that day and leap for joy, if it be for Christ's sake—it is a blessing indeed. Yes, if my faith shakes off the disguise, snatches the vizor from the fair forehead of the blessing, and if we *'consider it pure joy,'* (Jam 1:2) to fall into many different trials for the sake of Jesus and the recompense of reward that He has promised, then *'Oh, that we may be blessed indeed!'*

STUDY GUIDE

Blessings that glorify God and bestow His gift of salvation upon us are the greatest of blessings because they place us before His throne in worship.

As you come to this final study guide, make notes of the answers or concepts that interest you. Try to find similar themes or concepts in Scripture and then study them further. If you enjoyed the book and study guide, consider going over the previous questions one last time now that you have read the book in its entirety.

1. What is the source of true blessings?
2. How does Christ's work on the cross bless us?
3. How does the Spirit's work bring us blessing? Especially if it may wound or kill us?
4. What role does your Christian brother or sister serve in your blessing?
5. What other blessings does God give us to help us enjoy our relationship with Him more and prepares us for eternity?

5

A FINAL THOUGHT

Now, I will send you away with these three words.

SEARCH

See whether the blessings are blessings indeed, and do not be satisfied unless you know that they are of God—tokens of His grace, and truths of His saving purpose.

WEIGH

That shall be the next word. Whatever you have, weigh it in the scale, and ascertain if it is a blessing indeed, conferring such grace upon you as which causes you to abound in love, and in every good word and work.

PRAY

So pray that this prayer may mingle with all your prayers, that whatever God grants and whatever He withholds, you may be blessed indeed. Is it your joy-time? Then may Christ mellow your joy, and prevent the intoxication of earthly blessings from leading you astray from walking close with Him! In the night of sorrow, pray that He will bless you indeed, before the wormwood also intoxicates you and makes you drunk, before your afflictions make you think hardly of Him. Pray for the blessing, which if you have, you are rich to all the intents of bliss. And if you are lacking, you are poor and destitute, though plenty fills your store.

'If your presence does not go with us, do not send us up from here,' (Exo 33:15).

But, *'Oh, that thou wouldest bless me indeed!'*

REFERENCES

Christianity Today. (n.d.). *Charles Spurgeon.* https://www.christianitytoday.com/history/people/pastorsandpreachers/charles-spurgeon.html

Hendrickson. (2006). *Holy Bible. King James Version.* Hendrickson.

International Bible Society. (1984). *Holy Bible. New International Version.* International Bible Society.

Kid's Pages. (n.d.). *Aesop's Fables.* https://kids-pages.com/folders/stories/Aesops_Fables/page3.htm

Thomas Nelson. (1978). *New American Standard Bible.* Thomas Nelson

www.ingramcontent.com/pod-product-compliance
Lightning Source LLC
LaVergne TN
LVHW020425070526
838199LV00003B/284